PROPERTY OF

____

INSIGHTS

INSIGHT EDITIONS

San Rafael, California

www.insighteditions.com